SPENDING AND SAVING MONEY

by Meg Gaertner

Cody Koala

An Imprint of Pop!

popbooksonline.com

abdopublishing.com
Published by Pop!, a division of ABDO, PO Box 398166, Minneapolis, Minnesota 55439. Copyright © 2019 by POP, LLC. International copyrights reserved in all countries. No part of this book may be reproduced in any form without written permission from the publisher. Pop!™ is a trademark and logo of POP, LLC.

Printed in the United States of America, North Mankato, Minnesota

022018
092018

THIS BOOK CONTAINS RECYCLED MATERIALS

Cover Photo: Shutterstock Images
Interior Photos: Shutterstock Images, 1, 9, 13; iStockphoto, 5 (top), 5 (bottom left), 5 (bottom right), 6, 10, 14, 17 (top), 17 (bottom right), 17 (bottom left), 18

Editor: Charly Haley
Series Designer: Laura Mitchell

Library of Congress Control Number: 2017963373

Publisher's Cataloging-in-Publication Data
Names: Gaertner, Meg, author.
Title: Spending and saving money / by Meg Gaertner.
Description: Minneapolis, Minnesota : Pop!, 2019. | Series: Community economics | Includes online resources and index.
Identifiers: ISBN 9781532160059 (lib.bdg.) | ISBN 9781532161179 (ebook) |
Subjects: LCSH: Money--Juvenile literature. | Community development--Juvenile literature. | Regional economics--Juvenile literature. | Economic development--Juvenile literature. | Community life--Juvenile literature.
Classification: DDC 330.9--dc23

Hello! My name is

Cody Koala

Pop open this book and you'll find QR codes like this one, loaded with information, so you can learn even more!

Scan this code* and others like it while you read, or visit the website below to make this book pop.

popbooksonline.com/
spending-and-saving-money

*Scanning QR codes requires a web-enabled smart device with a QR code reader app and a camera.

Table of Contents

Chapter 1

Economics

Everyone has wants and needs. People use money to get those things. Money is a scarce resource. People do not have an endless amount of money.

Watch a video here!

People must decide how to best use their money. In economics, experts study how people make these decisions.

People need food, water, clothing, and a place to live. They want things like toys or movies.

Chapter 2

Benefits and Costs

Benefits are the good things that come from something. Food and water help people live. Toys and movies can make people happy.

These kids benefit from the soccer ball.

Learn more here!

People save money to buy **long-term wants**. These are things that people cannot buy right away. They do not have enough money yet.

People also have **immediate wants**. Immediate wants are wants that can be filled now.

Chapter 4

Making a Decision

Ann wants to save money to buy a bike. But she also wants candy. Ann has enough money to buy candy now.

Learn more here!

Ann has to decide. She could buy candy now or she could save her money for the bike. She cannot do both.

Ann decides she wants the bike more than she wants the candy. Ann decides to save her money.

Want	**Bike**	**Candy**
Benefit	Ann would love to ride a bike. Ann can use a bike again and again.	Ann is hungry for candy now. She can have the candy right away.
Cost	$100 It will take Ann some time to save up this money.	$4 per box
Opportunity Cost	The candy she could buy instead	The bike she could save for instead

Making Connections

Text-to-Self

Ann had to choose between a bike and candy. Have you ever had to choose between a long-term want and an immediate want?

Text-to-Text

How do the characters in your favorite books decide to spend money?

Text-to-World

What sort of things do people save money for in the real world?

Glossary

benefit – a good thing that comes from having something.

immediate want – a want that can be filled right away.

long-term want – a want that requires planning and saving for later.

opportunity cost – the things people don't buy because they're spending their money on something else.

scarce resource – something that people can get only in limited amounts.

Index

Online Resources

popbooksonline.com

Thanks for reading this Cody Koala book!

Scan this code* and others like it in this book, or visit the website below to make this book pop!

*Scanning QR codes requires a web-enabled smart device with a QR code reader app and a camera.